Bighead Anole Lizard on the Osa Peninsula

Books in the Wildlife of the World series:

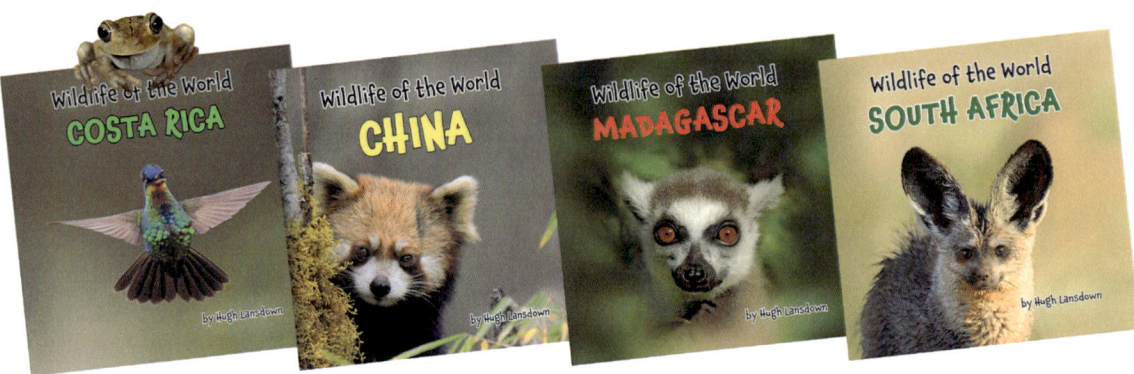

Wildlife of the World - China
Wildlife of the World - Costa Rica
Wildlife of the World - Madagascar
Wildlife of the World - South Africa

Coming soon:
Wildlife of the World - Japan

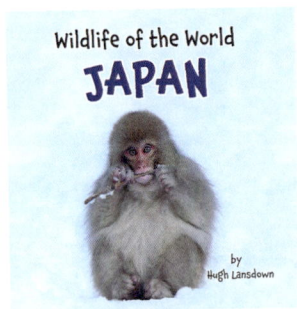

Visit *www.wildlifeoftheworld.com* to find out more about the books in the Wildlife of the World series.

Wildlife of the World
Costa Rica

by

Hugh Lansdown

Text copyright © Hugh Lansdown 2025
Photograhy copyright © Hugh Lansdown 2025
All rights reserved.
ISBN: 978-1-917175-13-5

Hugh Lansdown has asserted his right under the Copyright, Designs and Patent Act 1988 to be identified as the author of this work.

This book is meant to be educational, informative and entertaining. Although the author and publisher have made every effort to ensure that the information in this book was correct at the time of publication, the author and publisher do not assume and hereby disclaim any liability to any party for loss, damage or disruption caused by errors or omissions, whether such errors or omissions result from negligence, accident or any other cause.

The names given to animals in the book and associated online media are the most appropriate English names the author was able to find based on visible characteristics. They don't represent a precise scientific identification, which in many cases would require the animal to be captured and a detailed examination carried out.

SECOND EDITION published 2025
by Natural Planet Books
Unit 134893
PO Box 7169
Poole
BH15 9EL

www.naturalplanetbooks.com

Library Cataloguing in Publication Data. A catalogue record for this book is available from the British Library.

All rights reserved. No part of this book may be reprinted or reproduced or utilised in any form or by electronic, mechanical or any other means, now known or hereafter invented, including photocopying or recording, or in any information storage or retrieval system, without the permission in writing from the publisher.

To Phil

How to use this book

This is an 'Interactive' book, which means that as well as paper pages, it has digital ones containing videos, sound and slideshows.

How do I access the digital pages?

1. By scanning the QR codes

Throughout the book you will see Interactive Zones which look like this:

Just scan the black and white QR codes using a mobile phone, tablet or any device with a camera that can read QR codes.

2. By searching the Internet

If your device doesn't have a camera or can't read QR codes, you can just search the Internet for:

- **Hugh Lansdown photography**
- then click on **Books**
- **Wildlife of the World - Costa Rica**
- **Media Links**

You'll see a list of all the digital pages with the page number in this book that each one is linked to.

Wildlife Extras!

Some wildlife pages in this book have hidden animals that haven't been labelled. See how many you can spot then check the list on page 48 to see if you got them all!

Contents

	Page
How to use this book	6
Map of Costa Rica	8
Where is Costa Rica?	9
Regions of Costa Rica	10
The Caribbean Coast	11
Central Mountains	15
Western Rainforest	19
Northern Wetlands	23
Dry Northern Forest	27
Coastal Waters	31
Iconic Costa Rican Animals	34
Butterflies and Moths	36
Leafcutter Ants	38
Cloud Forest Birds	40
Capuchin Monkeys	42
Conserving Costa Rica's Wildlife	44
Wildlife Extras	48

Where is Costa Rica?

Costa Rica is a small, tropical country in Central America with the Caribbean Sea to the east and the Pacific Ocean to the west.

A line of mountains runs down the centre, where the climate is cooler and most of the country's five million people live.

It's over here... in Central America!

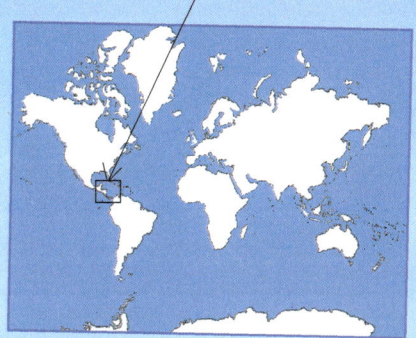

Despite its small size, Costa Rica has a surprising number of different habitats including cloud forest, rainforest, wetlands and dry forest. As a result it is one of the most biodiverse countries in the world, which means there are many different types of animal and plant living there.

Read on to learn more about them!

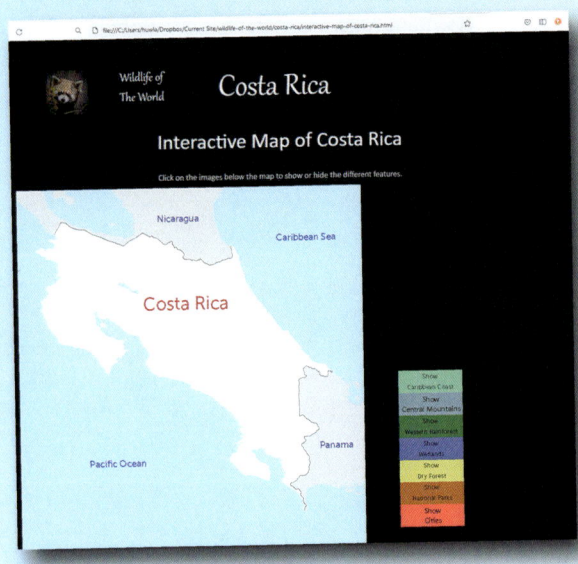

Regions of Costa Rica

Costa Rican people are proud of their environmental record. Theirs was the first tropical country to end deforestation, and over a quarter of Costa Rica is now protected by nature reserves and national parks, the most of any country in the world.

The main ecological regions are:

- The Caribbean Coast
- Central Mountains
- Western Rainforest
- Northern Wetlands
- Dry Northern Forest
- Coastal Waters

Try loading the **Interactive Map** and clicking the buttons to see the different regions as well as some large towns and cities, and the national parks where most of the photos in this book were taken.

INTERACTIVE ZONE!

Scan the QR code to explore the interactive map

(If you're not sure how, check page 6 for details.)

The Caribbean Coast

The east coast of Costa Rica is a hot, humid region, bordering the warm, shallow waters of the Caribbean Sea.

The tangled mangrove swamps lining the shore are a great place for birds like **green herons** to hunt for fish.

Further inland, tall, dense rainforest is home to tiny **strawberry poison frogs.** They get their name from their bright red colour, and a poisonous chemical in their skin that protects them from predators like the heron.

Strawberry Poison Frog

Green Heron

WHAT LIVES ON THE EAST COAST?

The east coast is the wettest region of Costa Rica with lots of rain... even in the dry season!

It is also the most remote. Not many people live there, and some parts can only be reached by boat. These wet conditions are perfect for water-loving animals like **black river turtles** and the strange **anhinga**.

Anhingas are tropical birds that hunt fish by chasing them underwater, but unlike most water birds their feathers aren't waterproof. Every so often they have to stop and hold their wings out in the sun to dry so they don't get waterlogged and sink!

Green Vine Snake

Black River Turtle

Anhinga

The beautiful **green vine snake** is perfectly camouflaged as it climbs through the lush, tropical greenery in search of frogs and lizards to eat.

Plumed basilisk lizards are only found in damp forests with plenty of water. They are also known as Jesus Christ lizards, because if a predator appears they can run very fast across the surface of the water to escape!

HOW DO THEY LIVE THERE?

Plumed Basilisk Lizard

Howler Monkey Resting

Howlers!

Animals in Costa Rican forests are often secretive and difficult to find, but not **howler monkeys**… as you probably guessed from their name! They have the loudest voice of any land animal and can be heard as far as five kilometres away!

They are the largest monkey in Costa Rica and roam the forests, feeding mainly on leaves and fruit.

Visit the Interactive Zone to listen to howler monkeys calling, or try the **Interactive Map** on page 10 to see where the Caribbean coast is located.

INTERACTIVE ZONE!

Scan the QR code to listen to howler monkeys howling

(If you're not sure how, check page 6 for details.)

Howler Monkey Feeding

Central Mountains

When warm air from the coast is forced up over the central mountains, it cools, forming dense clouds of mist... creating a special habitat called cloud forest.

The cool, damp conditions in cloud forest are perfect for plants such as ferns and mosses as well as insects like the beautiful **forest wasp** and **cydno longwing butterfly**.

These insects provide food for birds like the **black-cheeked woodpecker**. This male has just caught a long-horned cricket to feed to the young in its nest.

Black-cheeked Woodpecker

Forest Wasp

WHAT LIVES IN THE CLOUD FOREST?

Resplendent Quetzal

The endangered **resplendent quetzal** only lives in cloud forest. It is one of Costa Rica's most beautiful birds, and many tourists visit the country especially to try and see one.

Emerald swift lizards are also only found in the mountains, where they like to sunbathe on rocks and logs, but they'll dash underneath if a predator like a raccoon or fox appears.

Gray foxes will eat the lizards if they can catch them, and they're the only type of dog that can climb trees in search of food!

Emerald Swift Lizard

HOW DO THEY LIVE THERE?

Gray Fox

Four different types of monkey live in Costa Rica. The **Central American spider monkey** gets its name from the incredibly long arms and legs it uses to swing through the trees. Its tail is prehensile, which means it can be used to grab hold of branches and even pick up fruit to eat!

Spider Monkey

Cydno Longwing

INTERACTIVE ZONE!

Scan the QR code to watch some animals caught on a camera trap

(If you're not sure how, check page 6 for details.)

Caught on Camera!

Many of Costa Rica's mammals are nocturnal, sleeping deep in the forest during the day and only coming out to feed after dark.

These animals are very difficult to see, but can be studied by leaving camera traps out overnight to record their movements.

Visit the Interactive Zone to watch some mammals caught on a camera trap, or try the **Interactive Map** on page 10 to see where the central mountains are located.

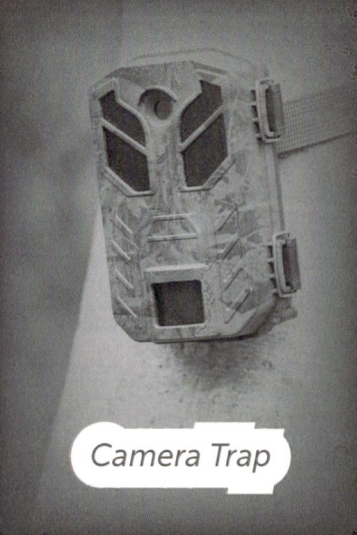

Camera Trap

Western Rainforest

The south-west of Costa Rica is very hot and humid with high rainfall... perfect conditions for tropical rainforest.

Many types of animal live in the western rainforest, but communicating with each other is difficult in the dense vegetation.

Male **anole lizards** solve this problem by displaying a colourful flap of skin called a gular sac, while insects like the **rainbow grasshopper** signal to each other with their brightly coloured bodies.

Rainbow Grasshopper

Male Many-scaled Anole Displaying

WHAT LIVES IN THE RAINFOREST?

Mother and Baby Three-toed Sloth

The most popular animals that people visit Costa Rica to see are probably the **sloths**. They are famously one of the slowest moving mammals... so slow that whole communities of insects live in their fur, feeding on algae that grow there!

Sloths live in the treetops, but there's an animal living on the forest floor that most Costa Ricans would prefer never to see. The **fer-de-lance** is the most dangerous snake in the country due to its large size and poisonous bite, which can kill a person if it's not treated quickly.

Fer-de-lance

HOW DO THEY SURVIVE THERE?

Tapir

Squirrel Monkey

Another animal that lives on the forest floor is the endangered **Baird's tapir**, the largest wild animal in Costa Rica. It is mainly nocturnal, spending the day resting in muddy forest swamps... a bit like a cross between a huge pig and a hippo!

All four of Costa Rica's monkey species live in the western rainforest, including endangered **Central American squirrel monkeys**. They live in large troops moving through the treetops in search of fruit, flowers and small animals to eat.

Riverside Wren

INTERACTIVE ZONE!

Scan the QR code to watch some rainforest animals feeding

(If you're not sure how, check page 6 for details.)

Feeding in the Rainforest

The warm, damp conditions in tropical rainforest are perfect for plants, so they produce lots of fruit and seeds for animals to eat. This is why rainforests have the most wildlife of any habitat.

Visit the Interactive Zone to watch some rainforest animals feeding, or try the **Interactive Map** on page 10 to see where the western rainforest is located.

Agouti Eating a Seed

Northern Wetlands

In the northern lowlands of Costa Rica, there are large areas of wetland. In the rainy season huge lakes form, and often the only way to get around is by boat. In the dry season the lakes dry up, turning into vast areas of marsh and mud banks.

In the daytime **spectacled caiman** lie motionless, sunbathing on the dry mud banks. As night falls they slide into the water and silently patrol around, feeding on fish, frogs and invertebrates like the huge, colourful **lubber grasshoppers**.

Lubber Grasshopper

Spectacled Caiman

WHAT LIVES IN THE WETLANDS?

There are lots of different habitats to be found within Costa Rica's wetlands, such as lakes, marshes and mudflats as well as damp woods, hedges and grassland.

This allows many different types of animal to live there, each making use of the particular areas that suit them best.

Ospreys are birds of prey that need big expanses of open water with lots of large fish. They pluck them out of the water using their strong talons, which have special sharp spines to help grip the slippery prey as they fly away with it.

Osprey

Green Iguana

Green iguanas are very large lizards that live in bushes and trees lining the wetlands, where they mainly feed on leaves and fruit. But as you can see from the photo…, despite their name, not all of them are actually green!

Proboscis bats feed at night on insects that live in the wetlands. During the day they like to roost lined up head-to-tail on the trunks of large trees that grow beside the water.

Collared peccaries are a type of wild pig common throughout Costa Rica. They live in large herds and like to feed in damp areas where they can dig up roots, seeds and small animals to eat.

HOW DO THEY SURVIVE THERE?

Proboscis Bats

Collared Peccary

INTERACTIVE ZONE!

Scan the QR code to see some more wetland birds

(If you're not sure how, check page 6 for details.)

Wetland Birds

Costa Rica's wetlands are famous for the huge numbers of birds that live there, with people coming from all over the world to see them.

In the dry season, waders patrol the mudflats in search of food. Then when the rains create deep lakes, thousands of ducks arrive to feed in them.

Visit the Interactive Zone to see different types of wetland birds, or try the **Interactive Map** on page 10 to see where Costa Rica's wetlands are located.

Black-bellied Whistling Duck

Dry Northern Forest

The hottest region of Costa Rica, with the lowest rainfall, is the north-west. The dry forests here don't have as many animals as other areas, but with less vegetation they can be easier to see.

The **ocelot** is a secretive nocturnal cat found throughout Costa Rica but rarely seen. **Cane toads** also roam the forests at night, but have a strong poison in their skin to protect them from predators like the ocelot.

Ocelot

Cane Toad

WHAT LIVES IN THE DRY FOREST?

With low rainfall and humidity, plants grow slowly in the dry forest, so it's much more open, without much undergrowth.

This makes it difficult for animals to hide, so they have to find other ways of staying safe. The beautiful green **lynx spider** has to lay her eggs out in the open, so she stands guard to protect them until they hatch.

Basilisk lizards run across water to escape from predators, but when the water has dried up its easy for predators like this **spiny-tailed iguana** to follow and catch them.

Lynx Spider with its egg sack

Spiny-tailed Iguana Eating a Basilisk Lizard

HOW DO THEY SURVIVE THERE?

White-nosed Coati

White-nosed coati are omnivores, which means they eat almost any food, from fruit and seeds to insects, lizards and bird's eggs. They mainly forage on the ground but are agile climbers and will head for the treetops if danger threatens.

The huge, endangered **great curassow** also feeds mostly on the ground, but will fly up to the treetops in times of danger.

Great Curassow

INTERACTIVE ZONE!

Scan the QR code to watch animals visiting a natural spring

(If you're not sure how, check page 6 for details.)

The Search for Water

In the dry season there can be long periods without any rain at all, and the forests dry up completely. Then the only water available for animals like the **tayra** below is from a few natural springs.

Visit the Interactive Zone to see some animals visiting a natural spring in the dry forest, or try the **Interactive Map** on page 10 to see where dry forest is located.

Tayra at a Natural Spring

Coastal Waters

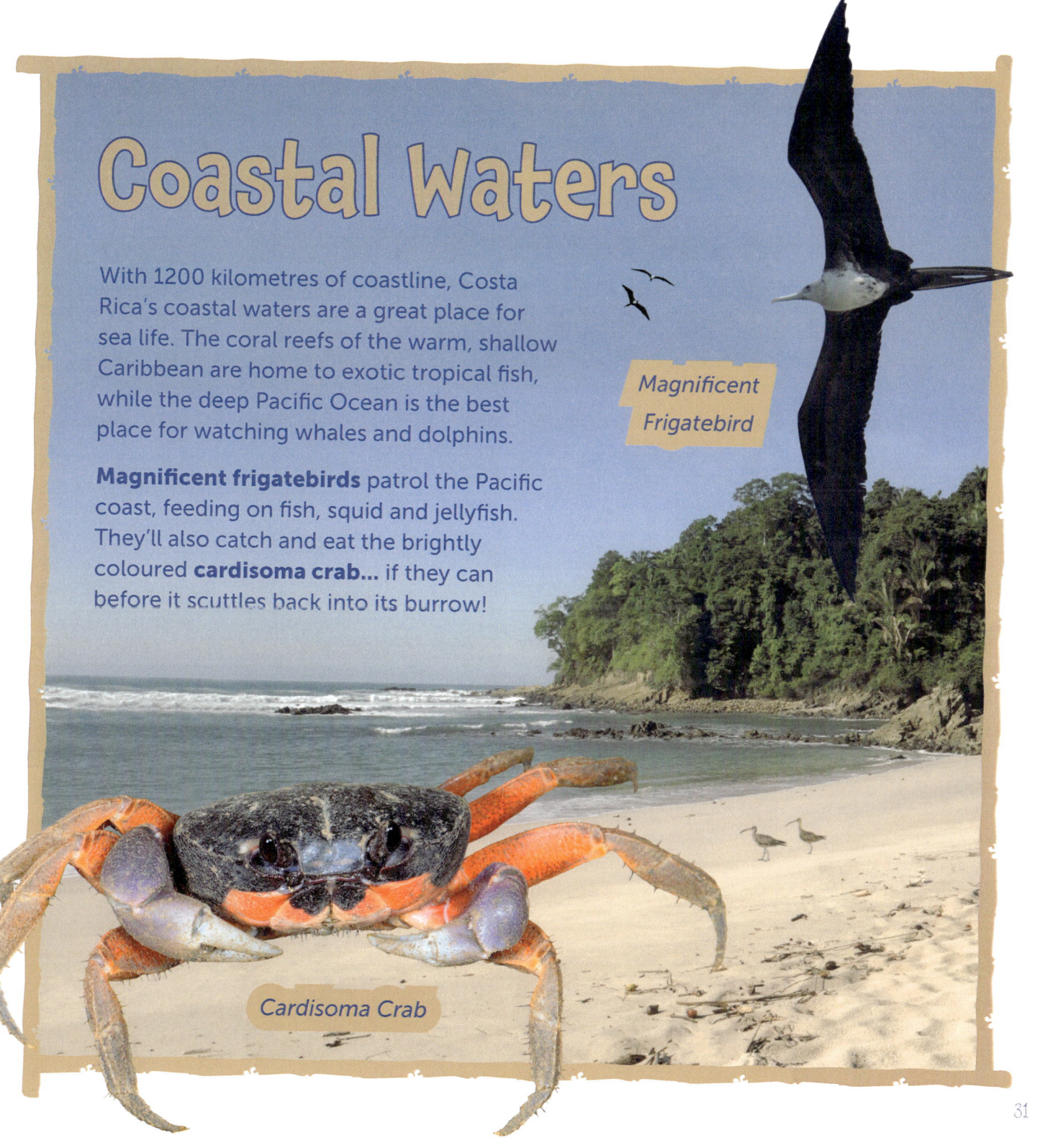

With 1200 kilometres of coastline, Costa Rica's coastal waters are a great place for sea life. The coral reefs of the warm, shallow Caribbean are home to exotic tropical fish, while the deep Pacific Ocean is the best place for watching whales and dolphins.

Magnificent frigatebirds patrol the Pacific coast, feeding on fish, squid and jellyfish. They'll also catch and eat the brightly coloured **cardisoma crab...** if they can before it scuttles back into its burrow!

Magnificent Frigatebird

Cardisoma Crab

WHAT LIVES IN THE SEA?

Many different types of sea bird live on Costa Rica's coasts, often feeding far out at sea but coming ashore to sleep and build their nests.

Brown boobies and **sandwich terns** both feed mainly on fish, which they catch by diving into the sea. Their feathers are waterproof so they don't have to dry them like the anhinga on page 12. Boobies stay all year, nesting along both coasts, but the terns are winter visitors from North America.

Humpback whales can also be seen off both the Pacific and Caribbean coasts of Costa Rica. They migrate from their cold feeding grounds to give birth in the warm tropical waters. If you look closely at the photo below, you can see a young baby swimming alongside its mother.

Brown Booby

Humpback Whales

Spotted Dolphin

HOW DO THEY SURVIVE?

Sandwich Tern

Pan-tropical spotted dolphins feed on small fish and can often be seen leaping right out of the water like this one.

Green turtles spend their whole lives at sea, except when females come ashore to lay their eggs on sandy Pacific and Caribbean beaches. They are endangered due to pollution in the sea, getting caught in fishing nets, and their eggs being illegally collected for food.

Green Turtle

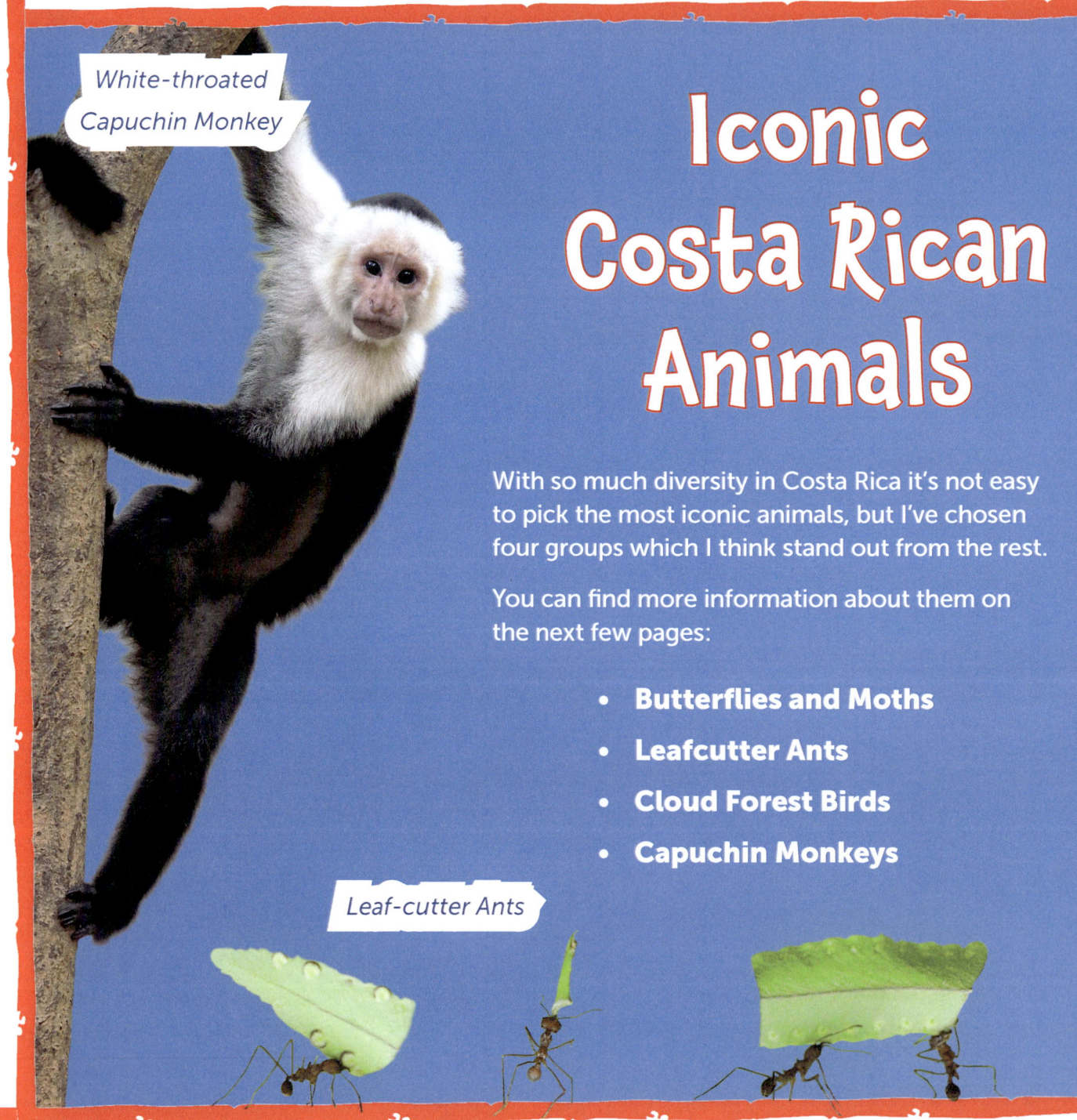

White-throated Capuchin Monkey

Iconic Costa Rican Animals

With so much diversity in Costa Rica it's not easy to pick the most iconic animals, but I've chosen four groups which I think stand out from the rest.

You can find more information about them on the next few pages:

- **Butterflies and Moths**
- **Leafcutter Ants**
- **Cloud Forest Birds**
- **Capuchin Monkeys**

Leaf-cutter Ants

Butterflies

Striped Blue Skipper

Costa Rica is a superb place for butterflies and moths, with 1250 different types of butterfly and over 8000 types of moth!

The **striped blue skipper** is a fast-flying little forest butterfly, whereas the **king swallowtail** is huge, colourful and roams throughout the country.

Longwing butterflies are also colourful, and their bodies contain a poison from the plants they ate as caterpillars... so predators leave them alone!

King Swallowtail

Hewitson's Longwing

and Moths

People often think that moths are small, dull insects that only fly at night, but none of that is actually true.

Many types of moth fly in the daytime and some are really huge. **Rothschild's giant silkmoths** are bigger than many birds... and even some mammals!

Moths can also be just as colourful as butterflies, as you can see from the photos on this page and in the **Interactive Zone**. Visit to see lots more Costa Rican butterflies and moths.

Rothschild's Giant Silkmoth

Acraga Moth

INTERACTIVE ZONE!

Scan the QR code for more Costa Rican butterflies and moths

(If you're not sure how, check page 6 for details.)

Leafcutter Ants

Despite their tiny size, **leafcutter ants** are some of the most facinating of all Costa Rica's wildlife. They have the most complicated society of any animal other than humans, and live in huge underground nests as big as a large house!

Cutting a section out of a leaf

Carrying a large leaf

Each nest is a complex community of as many as 8 million ants, each with their own particular job. There are gardeners, nurses, soldiers, foragers, construction workers and of course the queen who controls it all.

The society is based around farming, growing a special fungus which is the colony's only food. Forager ants go out into the forest and select suitable leaves to cut up and bring back to the nest. Huge soldier ants clear a path through the leaf-litter and protect foragers as they work.

Back in the nest, tiny gardener ants chew up the leaves to make a compost for the fungus crop to grow on.

The role of the queens, who can live as long as 20 years, is to lay eggs from which all the other ants in the colony develop.

Visit the **Interactive Zone** to watch leafcutter ants collecting leaves.

Carrying leaves back to the nest after cutting them

Carrying a red petal back to the nest

INTERACTIVE ZONE!

Scan the QR code to watch leafcutter ants working

(If you're not sure how, check page 6 for details.)

Cloud Forest Birds

Costa Rica is one of the most popular birdwatching destinations in the world, with over 850 different species. The biggest variety is found in the humid cloud forest. The beautiful **blue-crowned motmot** likes to perch in shady bushes, ready to swoop down and snap up a tasty insect snack!

Blue-crowned Motmot

Magnificent Hummingbird

Magnificent hummingbirds, with their brilliant blue throats, zoom from flower to flower sipping nectar, while **sooty-capped bush tanagers** roam the forest in small flocks searching for insects and fruit. The favouirite food of **acorn woodpeckers** is of course acorns, which they collect and store in holes in tree trunks.

Visit the **Interactive Zone** to see some more cloud forest birds.

Sooty-capped Bush-Tanager

Acorn Woodpecker

INTERACTIVE ZONE!

Scan the QR code to see more cloud forest birds

(If you're not sure how, check page 6 for details.)

Capuchin Monkeys

There are four different types of monkey found in Costa Rica (see pages 14, 17 & 21) and the **white-throated capuchins** are the most common. They roam the country's forests in noisy troops of as many as 40.

Capuchins are also the monkeys most likely to come into contact with people. They are omnivores, which means they eat fruit and leaves but also animals such as insects, reptiles, birds and even small mammals.

This varied diet, combined with their intelligence, means capuchins like to try and steal food from humans. They can often be seen picking waste food out of bins but will also steal from inside houses and cars if they get the chance!

Capuchins are some of the most intelligent animals in the world. In the past, thousands were captured and sent to the United States for scientific experimentation, and they are still sometimes kept as pets.

They are one of the few animals that have learnt to use tools, such as using stones as hammers. They also rub smelly leaves on themselves as insect repellent!

Visit the **Interactive Zone** to watch how some capuchin monkeys behave.

Capuchin raiding a litter bin

INTERACTIVE ZONE!

Scan the QR code to see more capuchin monkeys

(If you're not sure how, check page 6 for details.)

HOW ARE THEY DOING?

Conserving Costa Rica's Wildlife

Deforestation has been stopped

Costa Rica is one of the best countries in the world at caring for the environment. In 2019 it received the United Nations 'Champion of the Earth' award, and by 2022, nearly 60% was covered in forest.

They still face some issues though, as the growning human population brings people into conflict with nature.

With more people and traffic, more wildlife is killed on the roads. More farming means monkeys and wild cats are sometimes killed to protect crops and livestock. Some people take baby wild animals as pets, then abandon them when they get too big, like this puma at the Las Pumas Rescue Centre.

Rescued Puma

WHAT ABOUT THE FUTURE?

Aiming for 100% renewable energy

Some people still collect turtle eggs to eat, and with more people there is more pollution, like plastic, which is dangerous for turtles and other animals.

The Costa Rican people are working hard to solve these problems though, creating safe road crossings for wildlife and educating the population not to kill wild animals or take them as pets. They are also aiming to be one of the first countries in the world using 100% renewable electricity.

Let's hope they keep up this good work, so Costa Rica can continue to lead the world in protecting wildlife and the environment!

Turtle laying eggs at night

Index

Acorn Woodpecker 41

Acraga Moth 37

Agouti 22

Anhinga 12

Bighead Anole 1

Black-cheeked Woodpecker 15

Black River Turtle 12

Blue-crowned Motmot 40

Brown Booby 32

Brown Pelican 32, 48

Bullet Ant 13, 48

Butterflies 17, 36

Camera Trap 18

Cane Toad 27

Capuchin Monkey 34, 42–43

Cardisoma Crab 31

Collared Peccary 25

Common Black Hawk 12, 48

Crested Coquette 40, 48

Cydno Longwing Butterfly 17

Emerald Glass Frog 20, 48

Emerald Swift Lizard 16

Fer-de-lance 20

Fiery-throated Hummingbird 35

Forest Wasp 15

Frogs and Toads 11, 20, 27, 48

Gray Fox 17

Great Tinamou 20, 48

Green Heron 11

Green Iguana 24

Green Turtle 45

Green Vine Snake 12–13

Hewitson's Longwing 36

Hoffman's Woodpecker 28, 48

Howler Monkey 14

Humback Whale 32

King Swallowtail 36

Leafcutter Ants 34–35, 38–39

Lizards 1, 13, 16, 19, 24, 28–29

Lubber Grasshopper 23

Lynx Spider 28

Magnificent Frigatebird 31

Magnificent Hummingbird 40

Many-scaled Anole 19

Map of Costa Rica 8

Monkeys 14, 17, 21, 42–43, 44

Montezuma Oropendola 40, 48

Ocelot 27

Osprey 24

Plumed Basilik Lizard 13

Proboscis Bat 25

Puma 44

QR codes 6, 10, 14, 18, 22, 26, 30, 37, 39, 41, 43, 48

Raccoon 44

Resplendent Quetzal 16

Riverside Wren 21

Roseate Spoonbill 24, 48

Sandwich Tern 33

Silkmoth 37

Silky Flycather 16, 48

Slender Anole 16, 48

Smooth-banded Sister 35

Snakes 12–13, 20

Sooty-capped Bush-Tanager 41

Spectacled Caiman 23

Spider Monkey 17

Spiny-tailed Iguana 28

Spotted Dolphin 33

Squirrel Monkey 21

Strawberry Poison Frog 11

Striped Blue Skipper 36

Sungrebe 11, 48

Swallow-tailed Kite 16, 48

Tapir 21

Tayra 30

Three-toed Sloth 20

Turtles 12, 33, 45

Whimbrel 31, 48

Whiptail Lizard 29, 48

Whistling Duck 24–25, 26, 48

White-fronted Amazon Parrots 29, 48

White-nosed Coati 29, 52

White-whiskered Puffbird 21, 48

Wood Stork 24–25, 48

Wildlife Extras!

On some pages, there are photos of animals that haven't been labelled, usually in the background or hidden in vegetation.

See how many you can spot, then check the list below to see if you got them all. You can also scan the QR code above to find out more about them.

Page	Animals
11	A sungrebe swimming in the bottom right.
12	A common black hawk flying above.
13	A bullet ant on a leaf above the basilisk lizard.
16	A long-tailed silky flycatcher in the leaves at the top, a swallow-tailed kite flying near it, and a slender anole on a branch below the quetzal.
20	An emerald glass frog in the plant on the left and a great tinamou below.
21	A white-whiskered puffbird in the leaves above the tapir.
24,25	A roseate spoonbill and lots of whistling ducks in the marsh behind the iguana, and eight wood storks flying over them.
28	A Hoffman's woodpecker on a branch behind the lynx spider.
29	Two white-fronted Amazon parrots in a tree behind the currassow and a barred whiptail lizard in the leaf-litter at the front.
31	Two frigatebirds flying above the trees and two whimbrel on the shore.
32	Five brown pelicans flying behind the humpback whales.
33	Three spotted dolphins behind the turtle.
40	Two crested coquette hummingbirds feeding below the motmot and a montezuma oropendola to the right of the magnificent hummingbird.

Acknowledgements

Many people have helped me in writing this book, and I would like to thank some of them here:

Filip and Neilsy for guiding me around Finca Sueno de Osa.

Cynthia Bandurek and Marcello Carvajal for showing me frogs, snakes, lizards and insect life on the Osa Peninsula.

Jennifer Espinoza at Las Pumas Rescue Centre for advice on wildlife conservation.

Manuel Alan and his daughters for advice on where to photograph wildlife in Guanacaste.

Ulises Chavarria for guiding me around Palo Verde National Park.

Beth, Cat, Alice and Ellie at Rowanvale for their invaluable advice, support and patience.

All photos, video clips and sound recordings of wildlife in this book and on the associated web pages were taken by Hugh Lansdown in Costa Rica.

All the animals photographed were wild and free except for the rescued puma at the Las Pumas Rescue Centre on page 44.

Front cover photo: Fiery-throated hummingbird

Rear cover photo: Central American spider monkey

About the Author

Hugh Lansdown is a Welsh wildlife photographer who has travelled extensively, and his images have appeared in hundreds of books, magazines and other publications across the globe.

He is also heavily involved in conservation at home in Wales, working for local wildlife charities, carrying out habitat management work and giving talks about wildlife conservation.

You can find out more about Hugh's photography, writing and conservation work by visiting his website or signing up to his monthly newsletters:

www.hughlansdown.com/newsletters.html

Sneaky Animals!

A few random animals seem to have sneaked into the book when Hugh wasn't looking...

Page 2   - a gladiator tree frog

Page 3   - a three-toed sloth and a black iguana

Page 5   - a dusky owl butterfly and a cat-eyed snake

Page 6   - a damselfly and a saturniid moth

Page 7   - a roseate spoonbill

Page 46 - a red-eyed tree frog

Page 51 - a chestnut-mandibled toucan

What did you think of Wildlife of the World - Costa Rica?

A big thank you for buying this book. It means a lot that you chose this book specifically from such a wide range on offer.

We do hope you enjoyed it.

Book reviews are incredibly important for an author. All feedback helps them improve their writing for future projects and for developing this edition. If you are able to spare a few minutes to post a review on Amazon or Goodreads, that would be much appreciated.

White-nosed Coati at Palo Verde

www.ingramcontent.com/pod-product-compliance
Lightning Source LLC
Chambersburg PA
CBRC091205070526
44584CB00008B/335